ravens and romantics

mercedes paradiso

Books by Mercedes Paradiso
Estella and the Dream Traveler

Poetry
Ravens and Romantics
Thunder and Daisy

Awards and Recognition

"Shades of Romance" – Seventh Place, Single Poem Category,
20th Annual Writer's Digest Poetry Awards, 2026

"A strong, confessional voice powers these free verse poems...
A powerful collection...Confident, confessional, and confrontational
poems, cast in gothic darkness." – Kirkus Reviews

Published by Mercedes Paradiso, LLC.

www.mercedesparadiso.com

Library of Congress Control Number: 2025927685

ISBN: 979-8-9912170-4-0 (paperback)
ISBN: 979-8-9912170-5-7 (ebook)

ravens and romantics is a collection of contrasts, a poetic exploration of shadow and light, heartbreak and hope, solitude and connection. it blends timeless, vintage echoes of love and darkness with the raw, contemporary realities of modern life, creating a space where timelessness and the present coexist.

in ravens, the poems explore the darker corners of the human experience, where loss, sorrow, and pain take flight. *in romantics*, the poems celebrate love, beauty, and strength, reminding us that light shines brightest against the dark.

together, these poems reflect the complexity of being human, how darkness and tenderness coexist, and how even in our most haunting moments, there is a promise of light.

"It's my poetry. But don't let the cover fool you. It's a serious book of poems."

From *Estella and the Dream Traveler*

she traveled back in time.
in our dreams,
we had a meeting of the minds.
and so, this book of serious poems i made
from her thoughts in 2028.

for my family and
all the hopeful romantics
who embrace both
shadow and light

i poured the pain they gave me
onto pages 'til
i was free

contents

ravens

a five-month pilgrimage in,
my first message got a like,
the second one a listen, and
the third was left on read.
you are not a god, and
i am not your sinner.
i'm the one
who locked the gates of heaven
and threw away the key.
speak to the devil in me and
the devil will answer.

practiced manipulator,
callous seducer,
i knew you were an imposter
claiming to rule holy ground.
i was just the faithful
eating lies to save the damned.
thank you for the end.
your silence led him to me.

he speaks to my soft side,
the one made of kisses and lace.
you know that angel, don't you?
vamp nails over cotton candy lips,
fingertips tracing hips,
that voice lilting with grace,
full fantasy and honesty.
he speaks to the angel in me
and the angel answers faithfully.

-angels in the aftermath

you'll find my broken heart
in my poetry.
if my pain is what you're looking for,
you don't have to go searching,
it's written into my stories.
you knew exactly how i felt
when i saw you at your workshop
that first time.
didn't you see that
i'd dive into the abyss of you?
so why do you try so hard
to hide that lovely chaos inside?
i'm proud of the tears i spill
onto pages when i write,
my dancing like a fool, and
my lonely, burning longing
late at night.

-i'm alive! are you?

"hey, *guera*," my crush said to me.
too shy, i just watched him
from behind the barbed-wire gates
of the church downtown.
it was hungarian hour.
spanish hour came next.
in between the songs,
i never heard what was said during mass.
my religion has always been
the elements, beauty, music, and words.
church was time to shape stories in my head,
and the time before hungarian lessons
in the classrooms tucked behind the church.
no, i didn't go to bible study.
i skipped all the stories so many people know.
i learned another alphabet,
one with more letters,
two a's, e's, and i's,
four o's and u's,
two letters that count as one,
funny sounds most other american mouths don't make,
vowels with weight,
dreams in two languages.
i didn't know what *guera* meant at the time,
but i knew a lot of people did.
i was never like all the other kids.
to them, my ancient incantations didn't mean a thing.

-*secret code*

sparks whizzed by my face in the dark.
it was you who fired the shot at me.
it looked a lot like a roman candle, and
your new girlfriend laughed as if it were funny.
i shouldn't have helped you
by hurting myself,
drinking to the brink of death,
sinking too low by getting high
on that fourth of july.
tunnel vision brought me to my knees
next to traffic on the pch.
but the ground is where the foundation is laid.
it took years to build myself up, but
my new structure was made of impenetrable stuff.
i shined brighter than your firecracker
like i was some hot hollywood celebrity,
but you,
you'll never be free, and
your roman candles will never touch me.

-hard target

you tossed your sticks into a room full of people,
and i was the one to pick them up.
i was out of practice, and
it had been so long since i played music,
but i held onto them with love.
i stopped at another drummer's set.
"maybe, if i start with something easy,
maybe, if i just give it a try, i'll realize i didn't forget."
then you showed up and wanted your sticks back.
"those are special," you said.
i took a close look and realized
veins of glowing blue ran through them.
they were crafted with advanced technology.
"why'd you let me hold onto these?"
you had nothing to say.
that blue magic snaking through your sticks,
i'm filled to the brim with it.
you wanted to get some of that inside you.
where did she get it?
how is she filled with so much of it?
you wanted that glowing truth.

-you can have these back

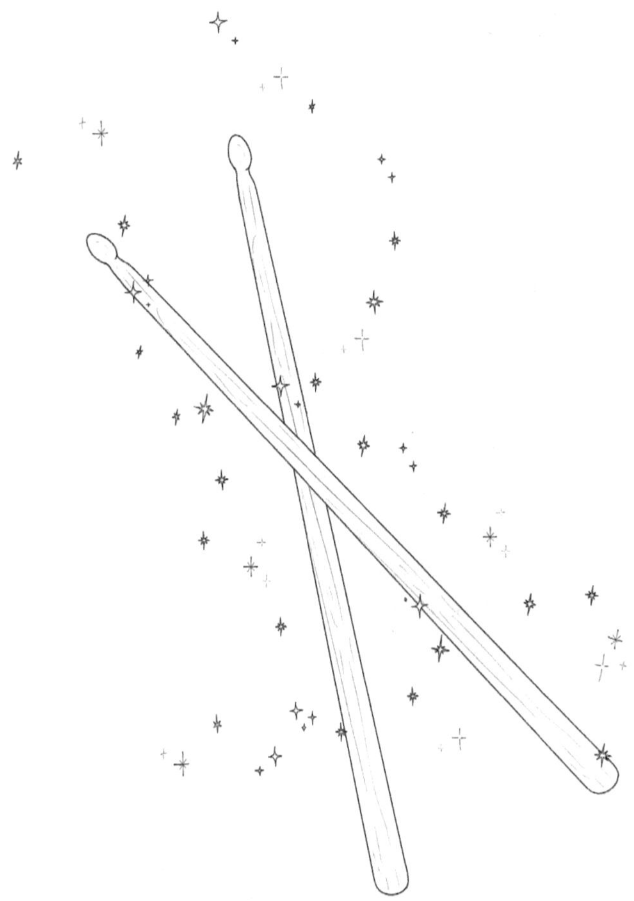

who does she think she is,
writing about herself,
everything she's kept inside
like she's supposed to?
she thinks she has thoughts
people want to hear,
that she can uplift and unite them?
the audacity.
how silly of her to think she has magic
that she can weave it into a tapestry
of the rarest love and otherworldly fantasy,
or curse the ones who cross her
with uncomfortable honesty.
does this witch really think she's
powerful, eternal, magnificently magical,
and wields some kind of alchemy?

-how dare she believe in herself

i felt like you were speaking lyrics to me
when "the promise" played at the end of the movie.
you grabbed hold of my hand.
there were things you wanted to say
but didn't know how.
there were no words that would make me want to stay.
but if i had, we would've spent weekends
sailing your boat around port ludlow.
we would've kept going to that restaurant with the funny hats,
raiding your neighbors' crab pots with our friends,
and eating my amateur berry crumble.
i wouldn't have had to see that look in your eyes,
the one that made me feel like every
villain in a movie,
face on a most-wanted poster, and
black sheep in a family.
now i'm the one who wants to make promises
to someone who doesn't want to keep me.
does he feel like the joker, jesse james, or
me, the black sheep?
maybe.
maybe not.
all i know is that
he's not thinking of me.

-napoleon dynamite

on my regular walk along the trail,
something unusual caught my eye.
countless vultures perched
on the high school bleachers,
like an unwanted truth had arrived.
they brought a resounding silence, but
i could have sworn
they were trying to tell me something.
i snapped pictures of the living gargoyles and
sent them to you.
"i would've walked right by them," you said.
it took me time to decipher the message, but
now i know what the vultures meant:
he bears no feathers,
he's not made for flight,
while he spreads darkness,
weave in your light.
they were right.
you're not my kind,
because if you were,
you would've stopped to listen to the birds.

-birdwatcher

i made it a daily practice to visit your gravestone,
the one you left inside me.
today, i lined my eyes with forest green and
dressed in black to visit your memory,
but instead,
i came face to face with fury.
i no longer wish to go wading
into those shallow blue waters of yours,
the ones that can't seem to hold anything real.
i'm deep in green, where the forest meets the ocean.
i've found my way back to where i belong.
here, the landscape stretches endlessly and
holds complexity that resonates with like energies.
paths lead into the unknown, and
those who walk beside me tread them fearlessly.
i finally stopped waiting for the dead.

-forest for the vast and bold

i didn't know that when you showed up
with your dutch freckled face,
mixed in peruvian,
rage against the machine taste,
and sandy surfboard
that i'd lose myself in you.
daring and cool,
you were everything i wasn't
until i met you.
so i followed you into the surf
at malibu third point,
got tossed around and spit out by the waves.
our love was a car without brakes and
when we crashed,
i didn't know how hard it would be
to get back my sanity.
i got lost trying to find myself again,
but when i did,
i was standing with paper and pen,
daring and cool in my own way.
i knew exactly who i was and
that i'd never go missing again.

-bigger than you

the cruelest thing you ever did
was share that song,
the first one you sent me.
you knew it was the spell i've been waiting to hear,
sensual and powerful,
vulnerable and visceral,
mystical and physical.
you knew it carried cosmic weight.
you dangled that song
like you knew what those words meant,
but you don't understand that language.
you slipped into the shadows,
lingering in the back of my mind,
and if i dared play that song,
you'd step into the light.
but now, when i hear those lyrics and that beat,
i'll be the one casting spells.
when those stars align, i'll share that song
to show that kindred traveler exactly how i feel.

-give me two weeks

check your dreams.
you may find those masqueraders,
revelers of deceit and hypocrisy,
who dwell in the in-between,
where misery reigns supreme.
he appears swiftly and
gives me the words i need.
like ghost notes, he speaks them softly.
he makes me think he's what i want.
he then tests me.
the golden mask slips and
i see what's real,
the stone core,
revealed.
he meets me in a dream and
cascades his velvety robe.
those aren't rubies of passion on that clasp;
they're lies.
that's no cloak of honor and the divine.
that's no dark knight's castle in the sky.
his throne rests in the in-between.

-not my ruler

the front door was open a crack,
light spilled in, and a breeze blew through.
so i panicked.
i could have sworn i had locked that door.
now, shut tight and secured,
i took my thoughts to my room
where i could then rest assured.
but in there, i got another jump scare.
the window i keep closed was propped open
with someone else's radio.
there was nothing left to do but
press play.
i heard your voice.
"all i want to say is i love you."
you're the one who left.
don't drop in on a dream
when you should be on the chase.

-get out of my headspace

terrain-altering winds are blowing,
the veil of smoke is rising, and
the fires of fear are growing.
something unprecedented is coming,
and the truth is going.
my feed is filled with fake.
is the hollywood sign burning?
i do a double-take.
the line between fiction and fact
is getting buried in plastic-perfect ash.
have our cities become battlefields?
i'm getting pushed into another box, but
i never fit into those.
so don't even try me with red and blue.
now, that's just another way
to divide me from you.
i believe in peace, equality, and truth.
what's happening to integrity and clarity?
where's my beautiful, uncomfortable reality?
i also believe in that crazy notion, empathy.
it can be found in that pearl of a book,
written slowly and painfully.
give me something containing
struggles and impossible dreams,
born from the minds
of uniquely flawed human beings.
i'm the master of my time, and
i won't let my attention be your commodity.
no lying algorithm can control me.

-*wicked winds*

the villagers with pitchforks and
my spells in their hands
chased me into the depths of the night.
they hurled words like stones
meant to destroy me.
they did not know that
i always carry a candle and
make my home in the dark.
i felt those words but
they didn't think i'd
cherish them as gifts.
the only lasting mark
is the castle i built from their
stones of bitterness and fears.

-witch hunt

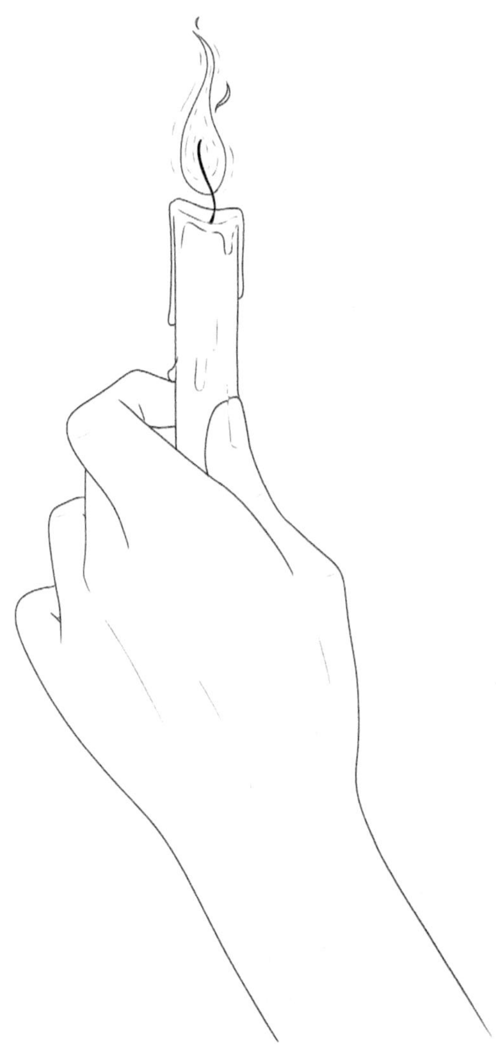

you asked about my story
with genuine curiosity.
i was nazaré and
you were the surfer
in pursuit of unruly energy.

i listened to your music
with a wonder-inspired intensity.
you were the ocean's choir
and i was the patron
seeking salvation.

you read me from the shore,
looking for the opportunity.
my love was the current
that swept you under and
fear was the wave
that dragged you back to her.

i lingered on that beach,
crashing at the break and
rolling stones in the wake,
advancing and retreating.
is that your song playing for me
or am i humming it from memory?

-is that it?

silence and distance,
they're your weapons of choice.
they give you the illusion of power,
but there are some things you can't control.
that sound you tune out during the day
but then keeps you up at night,
that's my voice.
you stay far away during waking hours,
but i seep into your dreams.
still, in that other realm, you tried to leave.
you didn't want to listen, so i had to scream.
as you walked away, i told you all the things
i never had the chance to say.
"you can't see what matters, what's real,
aren't happy or fulfilled, and
don't let yourself feel!"
then, i said, crying,
"your ten-year plan is a curated sham,
a life in a beautiful cage, but empty."
you turned and looked at me with owl eyes,
and in that moment, i knew you heard me.
i knew you felt that deep inside.

-closure

crows watch and wait.
they never forget faces and places.
they use whatever they find to make tools,
swoop on shady figures,
and speak a sophisticated language.
they're smarter than most people think.

between the stories you want me to hear
and those lips i can't kiss,
i'm listening, learning, and unraveling.
you think you're in control but
i see your true nature.
i'm smarter than you think.

-a crow you know

yesterday, you were a distant memory.
i saw a picture you liked online,
and i laughed, thinking
you're a thing of the past.
you disappeared so long ago
that all i remember is how you left.
today, a sad song escaped
from the box of you i keep locked.
i listened to it boldy,
knowing i don't want you, and
that you'll never hold me.
but then i slipped on the lyrics,
and fell into the melody.
out poured
your secrets,
your voice,
pictures you sent, and
all of your notes.

-damn your ghost

all it took was a glance
from him, and so many others,
to boil her down
like sugar and cream
into caramel,
and package her into
the right wrapper
in their minds.

she's small and compassionate.
so she's weak.
they didn't know she had been attacked
by those expecting scratches and slaps,
but she fought back with fists and kicks.

she keeps quiet.
so she's stupid.
they didn't know she wasn't saying much
because she was sizing them up,
that she'd never forget
everything they said,
that she'd put her pain into poems
and leverage those hard lessons.

she went to university.
so she's privileged.
they didn't hear the punk in her
before she'd spend endless nights
studying in her room alone,
that she was all but lost,
had to start from the bottom,
and fought for every grade on her own.

she got a good job.
so she's lucky.
they didn't see the grit it took to get there,
everything she gave up,
the countless interviews,
the hundred rejections,
her trying and her crying.

they didn't see the universe
she carries within.
she couldn't see theirs either,
yet feels their hidden struggle
churning inside.
that's why she's kind.
she understands and she cares.

but don't be fooled,
cross the line,
and you'll be met with
the kind of force
that shaped her mind.

-punk rock candy

i'm not that exciting.
maybe that's why i make up stories
full of magic and fantasies.
he got bored of me.

i must've been ten,
just a daddy's girl
with no friends.
that's when he got bored of me.

my voice doesn't chime
like the clinking of coins.
my eyes aren't as captivating
as three sevens in a row.
no wonder he got bored of me.

i don't flash and glow,
but observe and learn.
there are truths i came to know.

he doesn't love me and
she doesn't love me and
neither does he.
they all get bored of me.

-gambler's daughter

why did you put the book down?
was there witchcraft in there?
did you see someone between the pages?
was she deep and dark like the woods,
that place you go to think, dream, and
sit amongst the pines?
did the story spill truth
like an owl howling its secrets in the night?
did it remind you of something familiar,
a fantasy conjured with precision and foresight?
you dare not turn another page
for fear you won't forget that witch's name.

-scary story

the engineered moonlit glow
hides your fangs,
and your delivery is powerful.
it's how you'd like
the faceless masses to see you,
the humble teacher and
his groovy legacy.
i'm not like your followers.
they fell for a costume,
the one of a gracious guide.
i look at you with knowing eyes.
you're too weak to look within,
too cowardly to say goodbye.
your insincerity is disguised by
witty jokes and a charming smile.
who loves you?
do they truly know you?
have they seen what's in that soul of yours
and still lovingly kiss the wolf?

-fake face

from your room upstairs,
you hear the cupboards banging
when i make breakfast,
but you don't see me anymore,
not in the way that reminds me of the spirit
packed into this body,
the one with unruly waves and
eyes that aren't completely
brown or green.
i miss being seen
like someone's watching a movie
when i tell my stories,
as if i'm the main feature,
something real.
i turned into a ghost so long ago
that i don't remember you ever
looking at me that way.
but this house isn't one
the big bad wolf can blow down.
the snapdragons in the yard have mouths,
and they always say something kind.
peace lilies fill the house and
live up to their name.
our home's sturdy foundation and walls
hold me tight,
and so i keep haunting its halls.

-haunted house

i can see the hero starring in your movie,
the fanged warrior among the emerald trees, and
the symbols telling the world who you are
etched into your skin:
wise,

devoted,

strong.

that character glistens in the light.
but what about your
dark and ugly,
the things you've done
you wish you could set right?

wise one,
you're a musical master, but
were you humble enough to be her student
when you showed her the soft and lethal
duality that lies within?

devoted one,
you are loyal and restrained, but
were you faithful enough to hold the wild of her skin?

strong one,
you stand resilient in that frozen forest, but
are you free enough to face your villain
as your hero takes her in his arms?

i don't want your polished pieces.
give me the wolf or nothing at all.

-glints and tints

he put something in your drink.

what?
that's crazy.
my friend wouldn't do that.
i just moved to this city
without knowing a soul.
trusting, young, and dreamy,
it can be a bit scary
trying to make it on my own.
but i'm not naïve.
he wouldn't hurt me.
right?

wrong.

he put something in my drink
when i was an ember, but
i've grown into an inferno.
now, there's a darkness coming.
it's black, like a kind of magic
and a rogue wave in the night.
there's no use in running.
what's his is coming.
it's not governed by court or crown
but it's always on time.
oh, his downfall will be stunning.

-karma curse

i've been drawing the blinds earlier,
leaning into myself, and taking comfort
in the quiet lamplight.
looking within,
i've been thinking of you less.
we don't talk anymore.
it's been almost a year.
in the december stillness,
i cherish violet twilights and reflect.
it's when my words sound softer.
i think and don't want to post.
i used to miss your voice.
today's sun rose to a new year,
and now, i just don't.
last year, there was so much i wanted to know.
you were shadowed secrets, but
now i know that's for the best.
your mystery died in december's breath.

-new year's day

you were all floppy ears,
white with black spots, and
a heart-shaped nose.
but best of all,
you were mine.
it was real-deal puppy love.
i was the one who took care of you,
so i could claim you as my best friend.
i let you sleep on my boy band pillow, and
you ripped it to shreds.
i didn't mind.
you were perfect in my eyes.
until you ran away, so they say.
that was decades ago, but
when i think about it,
it still stings.
it was heartbreak of epic proportions,
the first big loss for my fragile young heart,
something that leaves a mark.
i never found another you,
not even close.
maybe i couldn't love them as much as you
because when you disappeared,
you took a piece of me, too.

-domino

in some stupid dream,
dripping with drama and mystery,
you told me you missed me.
you even said it twice.
but all it did was
make me into a virtual medusa,
betrayed and forged into fury.
if you really missed me,
you would've found your way to me, but
in real life, you're nowhere in sight.
the only thread that tied us together
was that fast-food substitute half-world online.
i don't need your face in my feed,
or your passive follow
telling me i'm not what you need.
so i blocked you and
restored my romantic heart's
savage version of peace.

-turned to stone

your beauty and glamour drew the masses.
they longingly reached for the dreams
that live in that heart of yours.
there were promises
of freedom, love, and hope
in your alluring landscape,
those enchanting tresses like amber grain.
but i didn't care for you too much back then.
a traveler full of fantasy,
i was drawn to the shores of far-off seas.
now your dream is battered and weakened,
an eagle spirit fading.
you're slipping from your peak.
but in your suffering
is where your glory comes into focus.
it's where i can see my love for you so clearly,
for i know that pain,
that longing for all you had and all you lost.
now is when i need you most, and only now,
i truly know what losing you would cost.

-*a fading dream*

on the first day at my new job,
when my unchosen adversary saw me,
she scrunched her nose.
that's okay.
i get that a lot.
some people think
they have me figured out
at first look.
that doesn't bother me.
i'll be your elle woods.
i'll keep my distance and
the questions to a minimum.
still, she made sure that
i didn't feel welcome.
at some team lunch,
i don't know how it came up,
but i said,
"my dad spends time at the casinos."
"my dad spends his time at the races,"
she said.
in that moment,
i knew she was like me,
trying too hard to be loved,
and she realized i'm not her enemy,
just someone who shares her
fancy suit-dressed insecurities.

-let's grab lunch sometime

like secret memories
under tahoe's moonlight on a december night,
poems rattle loose as i'm about to doze off.
i'll make them permanent tomorrow.
but what if one escapes and never comes back?
the room turns orange by the salt lamp's glow.

then there are my worries.
they're in endless supply.
are they dusted in my wonder?
if i let go, will some of that
magic disappear, too?

and then there's you.
of course, there's you,
all the other ghosts,
and mistakes i can't undo.

-reasons i can't sleep

as he played a quiet fade, she realized
they weren't going to meet at the workshop,
where they'd feel like teenagers again,
secret crushes hiding kisses.
he was never going to tell her
the story written on his skin,
so she said goodbye.
he was supposed to say, "wait, i need time."
instead, he planned his future:
overcast mornings, long walks with the dogs,
a life on the coast.
he made sure to tell her she'd have no part in it.
so when she knew there was nothing left to say,
he called her "the ghost of all ghosts."
he wrote a truth in which he doesn't have to feel,
but there is some truth in that version of his.
she is a ghost, one who will haunt him
because he knows what lives inside her:
love, fire, and his missing desire.

-*supernatural queen supreme*

who came to visit me
in the middle of the night
when i was tucked under the covers
with my fantasies and
you in my head?
i felt weight,
heavy at the foot of my bed.
did someone sit beside me
with intention and love or
was some sleepy madness at play?
i tore off the sheets and
peered into the black.
there was no one but me, and
my heart pounding in my chest.
i sank into my pillow
as i lay back down to rest.
then i felt someone get off my bed.
whoever paid me a visit had left.

-quiet company

there's a shadow in me.
i've come to know it well.
a shadow lurks in you, too.
you cover your ears when it yells,
you close your eyes when it appears,
but you know it's always there
like a cursed spell.
you think i don't know your shadow,
but we met a few times.
i know exactly where it dwells.
it shows me in the mixed stories it tells.
if only you got to know your shadow,
yours and mine could be friends.

-when dark sides dance

when you showed up, i turned you into a god.
crowned in laurel, you held up the sun.

your body turned to marble, carved to perfection.
don't think i didn't see the cracks.
i just filled them with gold.

this reality wasn't made for you.
you fell from your throne when
i stopped feeling valued.

i wouldn't let go of the idea of you,
as if it were music,
but isn't love itself.

when the space you left
began to feel more like a new beginning,
i realized
i was the one to put lightning in your hands and
wings at your heels.
i was the god.

i didn't want to say goodbye, but
because i forged thunder into the divine,
i had to.

-he gives lessons

turn on the charm and
reel them in,
like all their posts,
and they'll look past your sins.
whenever someone catches your eye,
that's how you play online,
but i see past your lies.
when i pick up on your pattern
and call you out,
you cower and hide.
turn the page in your playbook.
oh, look, it's your ghosting technique.
now your shameless game is complete.

-what's underneath

55

we danced in a garden of roses
in my dreams one night.
you said you were coming for me,
but then you said you were busy.
are you battling your demons, or
chasing the spotlight
in your poppy-covered california valley?
you said you want to read my poems.
instead, you leave me in torment.
does my voice scare you, or
am i just another one of your whims?
in another dream,
my love was that garden's bouquet,
and you were the vase.
you cracked under the weight.
so i showed up with flower-tied boxes.
i said, "don't worry,
they're just filled with air."
but my poems were in there.

-*unread*

all the ice cubes in her tea had melted
along with any warm thoughts of him.
under the harvest moon, she's free.
she no longer questions his feelings for her.
she pulls out her favorite cardigan, and
tucks her shorts into the bottom drawer.
she no longer posts stories
searching for his name.
he may have evoked a fire in her in august,
but for as long as she can remember,
she's always preferred september.
he's not who she's writing for.

-seasons change

don't give me a dispassionate heart,
like the clouds that chased me from seattle,
the ones that are a monotone canvas,
the ones that flatten
the city in gray,
the ones that put out my fire
and blur my words.

give me your light and dark,
like my favorite clouds,
the ones with definition,
the ones that hold
thunder and lightning,
the ones that put motion to the sky
and conquer mountains.

-storm chaser

some people know me as the troublemaker
who broke every rule in high school,
lost and looking to others for the script.
i had lessons to learn,
the kind they didn't teach
during math hour.
i didn't yet know my power.
some people know me as an attorney,
assertive and formidable.
i had something to prove.
i'm not that little girl
who skipped class to be cool.
thought i'd find what i was looking for
in that attorney personality,
but that was just more of my
"pleasing everyone but me" mentality.
i had enough of it and quit.
i became who i was always meant to be,
writing from my heart
for those who care to listen and me.

-you don't know me

i wrote you into a story,
one that carries my voice,
laced with mercy and danger.
it's for the manipulated masses,
the lonely, battered, and weak.
they'll find love in my verses,
but for those titans who exploit them,
i breath those words into curses.
i can't bear to read it again because
i've read it a hundred times over.
does it need fixing?
is it good enough?
am i good enough?
none of that matters.
the story is no longer mine.
it is yours and the world's.
it's meant to stir the hearts of mankind
and awaken the spirit of the times.

-the end is the beginning

we started like a movie
full of hope, one with a meaningful world, and
intoxicating authenticity.
we wanted to choose passion and life
over superficial monotony.
but we'd never turn those dreams into reality.
you sang over david bowie, cued the credits, and
played an entirely new movie.
you put cold perfection above all else.
there goes real connection, and
the exquisitely flawed sapphire of your truest self.
sacrifice what's truly great
to make it onto some famous list,
but time is bigger than you think,
full of buried, forgotten history.
hundreds of years is just a speck.
in that time, your face will fade.
this life you get is fleeting, but
you must sleep in that lonely bed you made.
you helped start the fire.
did it get too hot for you?
you created the cold.
did you feel that too?
hold on tight to your poison,
and fight your ongoing battle.
i don't envy that.
i don't need love
that gives me whiplash.

-*ego trap*

your world's matte black,
like your clothes,
your bedsheets, and
your soul.
i saw your mask slip from the start.
you called upon your students,
but then out slipped your "tsk."
he got under your skin,
that man who didn't raise his hand.
i knew you were fighting shadows, but
you used your magic
to infiltrate my heart.
"come closer," you said, but
"i'll never be yours"
was hidden between those words.
i told myself
i'd never let you in my head,
but then i felt that irresistible magic
on your skin that pulled me in.
so now i dream of raven sheets and
loving you in your black bed.

-*gothic fantasy*

life gave her broken voices that quelled hers,
those who wanted her seen but not heard,
high school boys who crushed her love,
then men who didn't deserve her trust.
she's gone to house parties in the valley and got jumped.
she's been in fistfights, kicked and punched.
she's been the target of jealousy.
friends envied her curvy waist and renaissance face.
lingering glances would send boyfriends into a rage.
she's been passed drugs at raves,
made fun of, embarrassed on stage, and stood up on dates.
she's always had trouble with authority.
corporate rules and hierarchies don't mean a thing
when all you care about is art, love, and living.
she had lost her way down some bumpy roads
before stumbling back to herself, her home.
but after all of that,
she found the voice that was silenced.
between the pages of books, she gathered new worlds.
she stored words in her mind and gave them shape.
she spun inadequacy and impatience into years of work.
she made her own fate.
her pain became a raven's call,
her scars, dark, dazzling feathers, and
she let go of the fear she held in her claws.

-raven heart

three stops to your heart, and
i couldn't get a ticket to train two.
i got lost at the terminal,
wandering around, waiting for you.
trapped in a romantic, antique train fantasy,
i filled my notebook with heartbreak poetry.
until i called to you from across the tracks,
rising above the screeching brakes,
my voice was loud, filled with love,
and trembled with emotion.
but none of that mattered.
you couldn't hear me.
your heart left the station.

-last stop

i'll move you with smoothness and
you'll find grace in my name.
you felt it after you cut me with silence and
i still held you in my embrace.
you're hurt.
i know.
you're lonely.
i feel it too.
you're ashamed.
it's okay.
i'll make that go away.
the sinners, struggling, and broken need me the most.
do you see the elegance in my divine empathy?
i gave it to you freely
before you turned into a ghost.
i forgive you out of love, not fear or need.
you don't deserve my kindness, so
i won't let you hold or have me.
i'm your lady of mercies.

-what's in a name

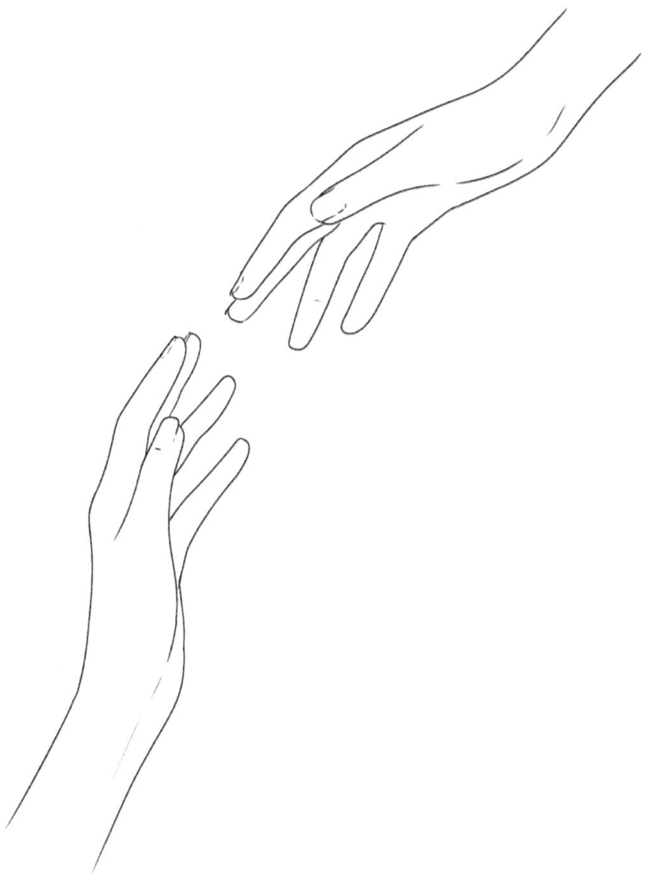

swooping and chasing,
they loved the game they were playing.
in a sierra diamond-dusted forest,
he made sure that the hungry raven fed,
and she returned the favor, telling the wolf a prophecy.
"i'm your lesson and you are mine.
that is our destiny."
he was convinced he was the leader and she the follower,
but it was the raven who led the wolf to the feast.
he likes the rush of new love and so does she.
blinded by that, she's a dreamer
who thought she found her match.
"don't you see that i am a wolf and that i belong to a pack?"
she ventures into the dark unknown and
her call carries messages meant to transform
while he's using a hunter's mastery to guide his community.
just as she foretold, there was something to be learned.
let the wolf be the wolf and
the raven be the raven.
their spirits belong to different worlds.

-the learned raven

romantics

my heart is tinged black,
the kind with texture and reflection.
i'm a raven,
matte sophistication but
under the moonlight,
iridescent blue.
look closely to see my spirit fully and
listen closely to understand my truth.
i'm obsidian,
creation through destruction.
the part of me tempered by time
was born by the fire.
i'm the night sky
where dreams conspire with possibility.
alive with stars,
there is light in my dark mystery.
but part of my soul is pink.
it's filled with petals and seashells,
diamonds and sapphires,
sunset blush and ballet slippers.
you bring out the pink in me,
dressed in softness,
elegance, and delicate beauty.
when you love me in black,
i'll wear pink for you.

-shades of romance

van gogh's brushstrokes never abandon me.
instead, they hold me dreamlike and tell me,
"i know your soul craves this kind of beauty."
his paintings are my sanctuary,
just like the museums and libraries
that have sheltered me,
welcomed, protected, and seen.
art turns me into a time traveler, and
music and books are my favorite ticket holders.
when i want to get really far from here,
beethoven and debussy take me to another century.
they dress me in lace and give me mystery.
when i'm hurt and the world feels chaotic,
frank lloyd wright's designs are a refuge of harmony.
i find comfort in his stained-glass geometry and symmetry.
and then there are the books.
a key to the magic inside us,
they save us when lost.

-my saviors

ART
ART

ravens, messengers between worlds, take flight.
this romantic has an encounter to keep,
one not meant for your black pearl eyes.
i meet with a vampire tonight.

on the edge of my dreams, he steers a ship.
torn by time's winds, majestic, and grand,
she's a moonlit, whispering ghost on the sea.

in his arms, i am home,
a pure and wild daisy under his hands.
hiding between his words are centuries.

we navigate a course of
passion and pain,
love and rage,
ice and flame.

he's a beautifully tortured sinner.
yet, i surrender eternity, bending to his bite.
he's my timeless, storm-kissed beacon.
in this ocean of darkness, he's the only light.

-lighthouse

sapphire notes play on my skin
as you drift to the small of my back and
pull me in.
on the dance floor,
we're pacific cliffs mist
sliding into a windy town's secrets.
don't you dare create any space.
that blue moon freedom on your lips
is all i want to taste.
the listeners, movers, and heat seekers
fixate on that sexy, slow tempo.
we're music flowing through speakers.

-with you in that jazz bar

you were a bad teenager.
that's what you told me.

you flirted with danger
and laughed at authority.
you felt too much and
couldn't control your emotions.
you fell into that young love
where you lost yourself.
you have stories about skipping town,
getting in trouble with the law,
fist fights,
theft,
lies, and
getting high.
you're bad and
that's your proof.

but I see
you're complex,
tragic,
full of life,
anger,
passion,
love,
kindness, and
mercy.
i know just who you are.
i see you when i look in the mirror.
you wear bad like tattoos,
and i love you for it.

-the bad ones are for me

light of brighton,
your shine
erases the space
disconnect resides.
fields of flowers,
satellites,
turning and tuning,
join in the movement.
i am a daisy
opening my eye
to the dawn.

-a new day

between business classes, i minored in dance.
only in movement could i find myself.
i could float like rose petals on water and
move like a karmic wind blowing romance.
music is more than sound.
it's a force all around me,
moving through my body,
making hidden parts of me seen.
i don't mind you watching.
my movements need eyes
like stories need ears.
i'm telling you things i can't say.
there's a little chaos and mischief inside.
but do you see the desire drifting at my fingers?
what about the dreams streaming at my elbows and
love flowing over my shoulders?

-*ballet in academia*

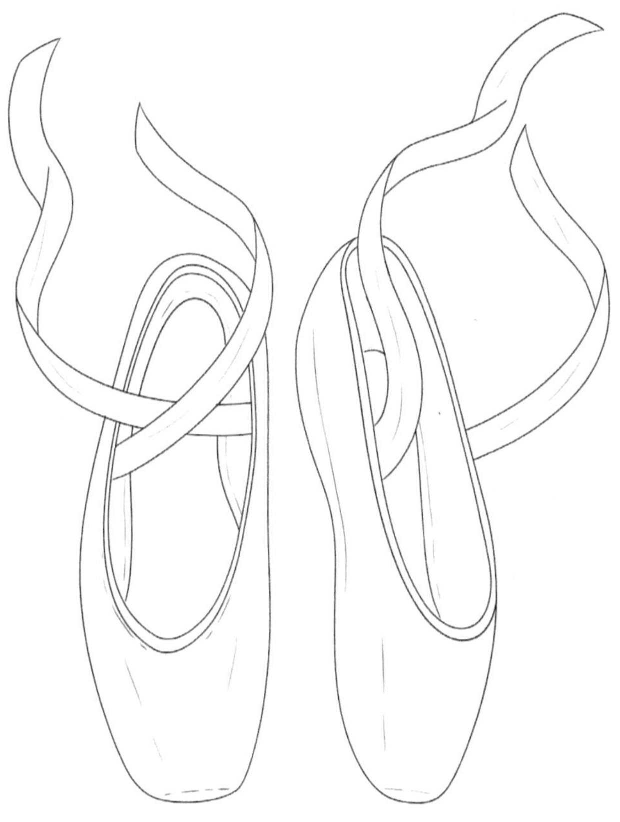

do you remember when
we used to hang out at the mall?
we had fun, just me and you.
like that one time i convinced you
to buy that outfit from charlotte russe
and you bought me a silver necklace
with matching hoops.
meet me at the food court.
we'll eat teriyaki,
plan an artistic life,
sip on orange slushies,
and plot our brilliant escape.
but then we started chasing empty highs.
romance novels came to life, and
instead of confiding in each other,
we nursed our own broken hearts.
lace up your docs.
we'll paint our eyes black.
we'll never be the same again, but
let's turn the clock back.
we'll watch the breakfast club,
rehearse half its lines, and
make each other laugh.
is my pendulum friend still in there, or
is she buried under all the in-between tragedy?
i won't let this life steal my youthful heart.
my axl rose impression and
horrendous fake british accent
need your attention.

-where you at, fool?

there are many places to grow,
shadowy brick buildings to scale,
broken stones to overflow,
sturdy oaks to twist around,
but my loving attention is warm rain,
a contradiction for the sake of beauty,
sparked infrequently.
my ivy doesn't flourish just anywhere.
but those rare times souls intertwine,
my love stands the test of time.
we may be met by cold and storms,
and climb in different ways,
but in the chaos, a tenderness remains.
my affection persists amid decay.
i'm evergreen coloring ruins,
eternally yours.

-love like ivy

the stars that burn the brightest aren't gold,
they're blue.
hotter than white-hot,
they don't ask for permission to shine,
they just do.
heavy souls,
they're no match for most,
but you can find them in twos.
the cosmos is unforgiving and cold, but
that won't stop them from making it home.
with their massive gravity,
they create their own black holes.
search their core, and you'll find
they're young at heart.
in the unending darkness,
they burn with the excitement of a new start.

-blue giants

i left myself with the crows on mt. diablo
to find that version of me,
the one bursting with creative energy and
gazing upon a horizon of possibility.
i drove seven hours down the 5
to get to the beach that held my dusty dreams,
that old home of mine.

"hey, mom,
the current version of me is all i can find.
where did we go?
you don't make your apple cake anymore,
you walk slower, and
your hair is white.
i don't dance like i used to,
no longer go out with friends, and
can't find that fire
that comes with living on the edge."

"don't worry, my dear,
you'll always find those versions of us in photographs,
and the version standing before me *still*
lives with freedom, dreams, and writes."

-*family photos*

shining in my rosebud eyes,
that's when the moon became my guide.
i used to wish upon it for love,
the kind in shakespeare's sonnet 116,
and for my dreams to come true,
ones that could be written into fantasies.
my eyes bloomed, and
my grand visions never left the sky.
i closed my blinds and
shut that cold moon out.
it came for me anyway,
finding its way inside.
it covers me in magic and lights me up in blue.
the moon didn't give me an epic fantasy.
instead, it reminded me that i'm complete, and
i get the stories meant for me.
i still wish upon the moon.
now i wish to keep the love i already have,
for myself and others.
after everything meant to destroy it,
my heart is still full.
my dreams are simpler, too,
and i tell the moon,
"thank you, thank you, thank you."

-growing gratitude

washed in orange,
i watched the horizon
as it held onto the sun
that dipped behind my world and
entered another one.
years before,
i sat on this shore,
different on the outside, but
my essence the same.
within that time,
i collected life,
like the shells I found
half-buried in this sand, but
that internal torch burns unchanged.
do you still feel like that curious child and
that trouble-maker teenager?
are you still trying to make sense
of the wild of your soul?
is turning life into art
still one of your goals?
we're apart but i haven't left you.
turn your head to the sun.
we are not born to be lost.
i'm not as i was, but
i am me in another form.

-energy persists

walking budapest's castle district one summer night,
i heard footsteps, and a song by the cure came to mind.
i wasn't in a dress or anything fancy, but
i could've been in a fairytale
wandering through fisherman's bastion.
lights twinkled off the danube like sequin stars.
the air was warm, but also heavy,
as if it carried a thousand years of passion and war.
that night and that place feel lightyears away, but
its gothic, baroque, and neo-romanesque live in me.
i carry an architectural mosaic in my memory.
from here, i can't feel the uneven cobblestones under my feet,
hear the violins, or reach out and touch the storied buildings.
but if i close my eyes, i remember that budapest feeling.
if a little piece of every place we visit becomes a part of us,
my bit of budapest holds the deepest love.

-gótikus magyar szívem

a fisherman lowers his line.
in the distance, he sees
the siren of crescent cove on the shore.
she leaves footprints in the sand
with certainty.
her song carries gravity and
a hint of melancholy.
moved by her voice,
he spills his bucket of rockfish.
"what have you done?
i worked so hard for these,
you witch."
"follow me," she calls.
instead, he turns his back and leaves.
later that night,
he hears her sing in his dreams,
and when dawn nears,
he returns to the beach.
no line,
no fish,
just him wading into the sea,
swimming after his witch.

-moon's pull

i'm the inkblot on the parking lot,
waiting for the bell to ring.
i'm words looking for a purpose,
misshapen darkness,
hoping to catch your eye.
maybe you'll wave, but
i'd give anything for a smile.
i spot you in the distance,
shining over the horizon of cars,
like you're the gold fire of the sun.
how do you burn like that?
i don't think you realize
i see a multitude of stars
in jeans and a baseball cap.

-brighter than anyone

october arrives, and i bloom.
like autumn leaves,
i'm full of warmth in shades of orange and gold.
my passion turns a deeper red.
it's fire at my fingertips
as i envision a new world to build.
i walk the fine line that divides realms
as magic sparks in the air.
like fall, i'm most alive
when i'm closest to the other side.

-*'tis the season*

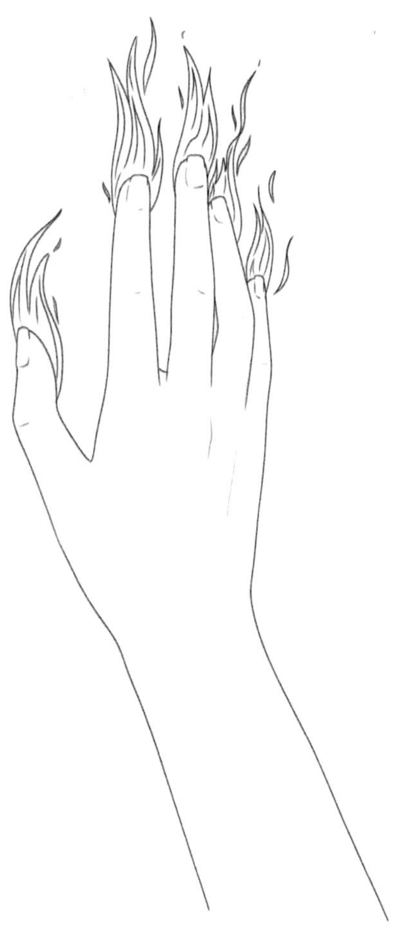

we were three women
in a black, souped-up camaro,
leaving an uninspiring scene.
no, we don't want your drinks and
we don't care about your politics.
my sister in ripped jeans was in the back seat.
dee was at the wheel, and
i was the shark by her side.
black sabbath's paranoid blasted from the speakers.
you could hear boredom and danger in our hollers
as we fishtailed it.
the wind barely tangled our hair
when red and blue lights flashed.
the guys we left behind
did nothing but laugh.
the officer got out of her car and
showed us her badge.
she heard their contempt and
took a good look at us misfit flowers.
"nice car," she said, and
glanced back at them boys.
"have a good night."

-lady justice

love the skins we're in.
we'll never be quite like this again.
change makes us beautiful
while we store what's eternal.
until we shine in endless galaxies,
our bodies keep our energies.
so kiss me fast because
these lips won't last.

-fleeting feels

i was born an artist,
and i'll die an artist.

it's in my obsession
with the beauty of humanity
and the natural world.
it's in my drawings,
the way i dance, sing,
and feel music.
it's woven into the way i speak
and the words that make up my stories.
my work is a painting
of how i see reality.
i'm inseparable from creativity,
and for this,
the world has punished me.
so i traveled down paths that
led me from myself.
but the artist endures,
restless, unyielding,
a force that prevails.
it laid me in ruin,
burned down every façade i built.
the faster i ran,
the louder it called.
i knew i had to listen;
i knew i had to write.

i was born an artist,
and this is why i'll die an artist.

-self-acceptance

you're the dangerous one,
not the flighty fantasies.
you're the quiet, constant,
unassuming, unconditional love,
the one to build a wall between.
we've been humbled by half-pints,
built an unseen empire, and
watched each other get older.
so we'll no longer carry the weight
of the institution on our shoulders.
we'll put away your rings,
choose our own jewels, and
wear them as spells if we want.
we design this house.
we choose our titles.
we'll take acceptance and understanding
over worshipping false idols.

-great expectations

dreams take me to depths i've never been.
they show me what i don't yet understand.

in the dead of night,
i woke to tears spilling down my cheeks,
heavy with awe and relentless.

you guided me through the station.
"i'm from here," i said.
your hand brushed mine and
i was hit with an otherworldly rush,
stunned by unfathomable energy.
"then you don't have to do too much.
you're no tourist," you said.
"yeah, i'll just enjoy the sun."
so you took my hand in yours,
and with that touch,
you led me to depths
my waking mind can't comprehend.
your hand slipped from mine.
without a word, you turned and left.
i felt the sun and didn't want it to end.

-touched by the sun

there's a soft closeness you don't get
when coordinating pet care,
color-grading your videos, or
even in the connection you feel to your music.
it's the kind of closeness that shows up
with the gentle touch of a hand
that melts that ever-present hard edge
you can't seem to shake otherwise.
it's the closeness you feel in a kiss
that erases every story you told yourself
about why you can't be loved.
it's how it feels to be looked in the eyes
by someone who sees past the public persona,
to the wolf underneath, and
still wants you
with the burning aliveness
of the birth of a new star.

-in her hands

i had a boyfriend, but you'd still greet me
with that bright look in your eyes,
back when you wore thick glasses and
i didn't think to make you mine.
i went to some of your shows at the whisky.
after that, you got famous and
represented regret and missed opportunity.
you went on tour and sold out stadiums,
while i lived my average life.
i couldn't listen to your songs on the radio.
you were everything i wanted to be,
creating something with purpose,
artistic and free.
instead, i studied business and
stifled my creativity.
but i got bolder
when time caught up with me.
i listened to your songs with nostalgia and
even studied your drum beats.
pardon me, but
i'm not looking for y2k fame.
if you have a look in my books,
you'll find new worlds built with courage,
not that girl full of fear, uncertainty, and shame.

-shadow work

a new dawn is coming.
rise with me from the ashes of self-doubt.
witches are blooming like it's spring, and
i'm holding a bouquet of reckoning.
do you feel small?
that doesn't belong here.
don't forget, we're unending and powerful.
where is your voice?
join me in song.
are you tired of living in fear?
together, we are strong.
don't be fooled,
we are not enemies.
we share the tragedy and magic of humanity.
there's no need to measure up.
it's time for our awakening.
love and acceptance are enough.

-era of the witch

cut it short,
and while you're at it,
tell me some jokes.
someone's living on them ends,
and he needs to go.
there's also some regret in there, and
please cut out that shame and sorrow.
i love the feel of that fine-tooth comb,
eliminating the lingering longing
as it glides through my strands of gold.
now, get the hair dryer and round brush.
we're going marilyn monroe.
you made me feel lighter.
can you tell from my smile?
do you see that i'm new again?
i'm walking around on a sweet high
with something magnetic in my eyes.

-fresh cut

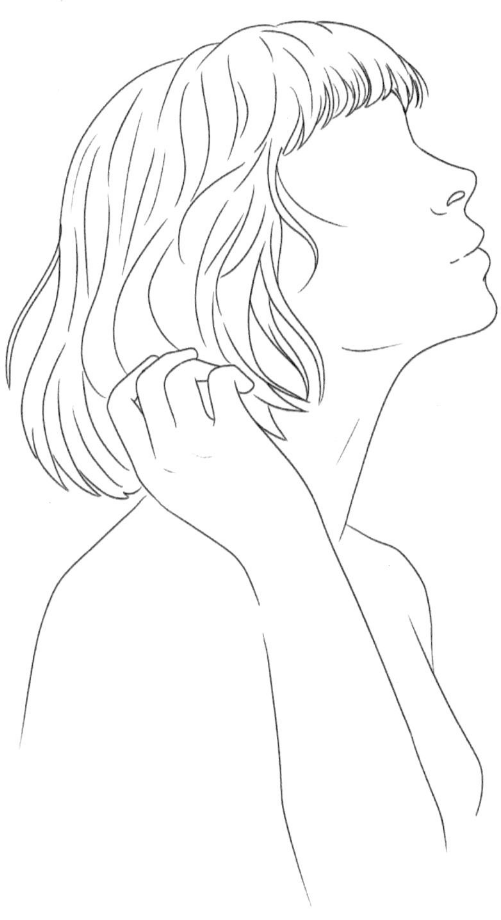

the sky tears apart and cries,
it screams thunder,
its passion cracks the sky,
and i come alive.
stir that fiery, familiar part of me.
show me what you got.
brighter!
louder!
i want to see what's in that soul.
what words are ready to spill
from those heavy clouds?
what kind of music plays
inside that mind?
what demons hide
in those dark skies?
those are my winds
keeping that heart warm.
you won't truly know peace
without dancing in the storm.

-show me your thunder

this world isn't it.
there's another one
on the other side of the sun.
if one realm is all you see,
you're missing the possibilities,
the creation of spaces
built with your mind.
there's also that eternity
where you can paint
your own sky
whatever color you want.
neon orange?
cool.
do you feel stuck?
you can change.
yes, you can.
are you scared of death?
existence is a tricky test.
but please,
treasure life as the ultimate quest.
we're everlasting, and
after a traveler's journey,
we all wake up.

-precious quest

i had never seen fog so thick.
if you've ever been enveloped by
the pea soup kind,
this was it.
the sun had just set, and
zuma beach
pulled a blanket over itself.
we peeled off our clothes
with urgency and stealth.
there were others close by,
but we didn't pay them any mind.
they couldn't see past their noses,
but sure heard us laugh.

-streaking on the beach

i don't need proof.
in the constellation of flowers,
birds' feathers, and fruits,
there is design.

i don't need to see it
to believe it.
i know our pocket watch eyes were
carefully crafted with time.

i don't need a church.
i've seen heaven in my dreams, and
the song of the sea and sierras
can take me there.

i don't need one word from you,
though there are secrets in that blue.
i read them using some hidden rhythm.
there's a novel in your stare.

-evidence

i know a lone pine,
firmly planted in the distance,
like it's stuck in time.

with its evergreen leaves,
all its seasons
look the same.

but that storm on the horizon is me,
and that wind shaking its branches
carries my name.

i'm made of movement,
spark fires, and
grow high into the sky.

with my ear to the other side,
i know the secrets buried
along with your roots.

don't be ashamed of the scars
underneath that bark.

from me, dear pine,
you don't ever have to hide.

-pining

i'll hike the trails of muir woods and
walk along the beach at dana point with you.
maybe we'll spot a red-shouldered hawk
perched on a redwood tree,
or watch a formation of pelicans
soar over the ocean.
we'll talk about what we see, and
remember the beauty.
but when i venture into nature alone,
something sacred happens.
my senses awaken with vampiric clarity.
i find answers in the forest's canopy, and
the wind on my skin feels like delicate electricity.
the birds don't just sing,
they make me angelic,
sharing secrets of what's coming.
this is a place where crashing waves become poetry,
and words unfold into stories.

-paranormal leaves and ocean breeze

give me a moment of your time.
i'll paint it every shade of blue and
spin it into fantasy.
it'll play out like a movie in my mind.
it was just a conversation, but
i heard all its vibrations and
saw its hundred layers.
your high-top vans, tangled hair, and black nails
told me you play guitar at midnight.
your dad parked his car in the yard.
you wanted him to stay but
worried about upsetting your girlfriend.
so sweet.
i ate your words like candy.
all you need is a little time with me.
put away your fangs.
don't worry too much
about your legacy.
you'll live forever
in my poetry.

-i'll make you immortal

i couldn't find you in the crowd,
not at first.
in a blur of faces, i saw two suns,
closed my eyes, and
they burned within my mind.
they were shining with intensity,
and too bright to be blue.
but i knew it was you.

my eyes are many colors,
gold, green, and brown.
they don't have your blue,
but at the center,
our eyes are the same,
black and burning
with love, rage, drive, and life,
like a fire in the dead of december.

-the light behind our eyes

in your presence,
i'm a waxing crescent,
building to a fullness.
you pour into my space,
new passion filling its place.
my heart is complete on its own,
but when we communicate
through symbols and lyrics,
it overflows.

-man in the moon

the beauty of a summer peach,
the poetry of its
sweet fragrance,
enticing and enlivening.

the beauty of a new fall,
the poetry of its
fiery leaves,
transforming and dazzling.

the beauty of a dark, frozen night,
the poetry of its
lonely silence,
heavy and encompassing.

the beauty of him,
the poetry of his
eyes full of longing,
endless and unfulfilled.

-spring's new beginning

we met when the weather turned warm.
i shed my well-worn sweats and put on a new dress.
i wanted you to think i'm pretty.

we skipped stones on donner lake,
and i read you my poems.
i wanted you to think i'm extraordinary.

you weren't like the ones who lied and left.
you weren't like the rest.
i wanted you to think i'm worthy.

you reminded me i'm all these things.
when there's no one i care to impress,
sometimes i forget.

-someone to impress

cornered by my phone
when i'm alone,
i get trapped in my apps,
that place with so much to see
it seems as big as the universe.
but despite its vastness,
i'm confined and uneasy.
i struggle to break free
until i step outside.
under a magnolia tree,
i close my eyes,
take a deep breath, and
listen to the wind in its leaves.
only then can i find that door
to the worlds inside my mind
where i can truly be free.

-the doors in between

there's an energy out there
that i recognize
among the crashing waves
and gulls' cries.
it beats in my chest
and flows through my veins.
there are paradoxes of
softness and violence,
allure and danger,
shared between us.
why couldn't we be lakes,
still and unbothered,
constant and sure?
instead, we're movement and change.
our waters' shades of blue fluctuate
and hide truths in their depths.
if we were lakes,
our guardians would be pines,
rooted and stoic,
but we draw sand,
shifting and unsettled.
standing on your shore,
we are restless and alive.

-icelandic tides inside

play your music for me,
something haunting and smooth.
i'll feel your heartbeat in those waves of rhythm.
move me like dripping honey, so i feel it in my soul.

lie under the stars with me.
i'll trace a path
from the seven sisters to the glow of sirius,
a long winding road paved with stories i've told.

let's set sail with no destination.
tomorrow's currents and
the hands of wind will be our guides.
a golden treasure awaits in our minds.

take my hand and come away with me.
there's a starlit world of our making waiting for us.
let me pull you out of this illusion of reality.
our honey-dripping story is where we're free.

-bohemian

i wouldn't have gone to the party
but i knew you'd be there.
i showed up with freshly painted cherry nails
and a black heart pinned into my hair.
trying my best not to notice you,
i chatted with some other moms,
then took my snacks and sat with a group
on the other end of the backyard.
sliding into one of the open chairs,
you joined us, and
the voices of the others
seemed to fade.
every move you made
was sun glinting off glass.
every word you said
were radio waves in space.
we all had stories,
but i only heard yours.
when i spoke with the group,
whatever i said was for you.
when i asked you about your dad
and your eyes landed on mine,
everyone around us disappeared
along with my reasonable mind.

-party of two

like my grandma's vintage playing cards,
i shuffle my thoughts.
suits of acorn, pumpkin, oak, and heart,
i hold them close to study.
the world, like cards, is full of symbols.

words, acorns of my mind,
planted by touch, curiosity,
art, and adversity,
need time to grow into something mighty.

under the harvest moon,
my story blooms in your heart.
you gather me,
your orange autumn jewel, and
light me from within.

along the iron horse trail,
the ravens hide among the oaks.
together, they stand strong and
share with me their wisdom.

and in it all,
the silver-blue of day's first light,
puzzle pieces in my dreams,
voiceless visitors and their secrets,
i watch,
i listen,
i notice.
there are signs.
they spell change, and
all of them echo your name.

-in the cards

in music,
there's no one to conquer.
do you feel it connecting us?
it doesn't divide.

jazz, rock, and folk,
keep the guitar strokes and
leave greed out,
so there are no wars.

play me a melody,
something to forget
politics and tragedy.
sing it loud.
give it some poetry.

the devil's not in the lyrics.
it's in the mouths of tyrants,
the insatiable and vicious.

so pick up your bass.
i'm on my feet.
we're in control.
your voice shakes souls.
there's something in it,
rage, truth, and spirit.

-in music we trust

i put a part of me on paper,
a book of spells
that speaks a story of timeless love and
a battle between heaven and hell.
it led you to me,
a map of energy and resonance
containing all of your requirements,
beauty, purity, and honesty.
have i passed your test,
or do you need more evidence?
like a glowing blue face tattoo,
my story of love, magic, and truth
is a lasting mark for all to see.
do you know me now,
or do you need more proof?

-find me in fiction

141

i don't need to be chosen,
for i know that
the love in my heart
rises over an empty sea.
it's that lighthouse,
enduring like the stars.

i'm not pining for awards,
for i know that
there's a fire in me.
its fuel is made of
meaning, truth, connection
and a haunting harmony.

i don't need bright lights,
applause, and big stages,
for i know that
my stories spin dreams
in those caught in its pages.

i'm not wishing
to make your list of the greats,
for i know that
my soul is free.
i didn't need your permission
to create new worlds,
or simply be me.

-intangible valuables

my will does not allow
"the end" on the last page
to have its final say.
it will find more ivory sheets
to carve its inky river of desire.
it doesn't speak quietly
when it has a message to convey,
and it doesn't speak politely
when opposing forces get in its way.
it comes looking for my peace,
grabs my wrists, and
pulls me from my seat of ease.
it puts my hands where they're meant to be,
typing with that fuel that burns endlessly.
no, there is no cozy end,
not just in stories,
but at every waking bend.
it'll follow me across the veil,
where it will continue to sing
with the fury of a coming reckoning.
can you hear it in my voice?
just like the softness, sadness, and fire,
there is no hiding it.
can you see it in my eyes?
they give away that will
that rages deep inside.

-infinite will

there's a part of my childhood
that's a ballerina music box
full of fireflies, lilies of the valley,
samples from the cheese shop on austin street,
and peter's backyard full of car parts.
there were long elevator rides to the top floor,
nightmares about tigers, and there was city life.
just learning how to really move in ballet class,
i was the only weirdo dressed in red tights.
but i had never been so free as when
i rode my bike on my own through queens.
find me in that black and white photo.
i'm the one with sad eyes in sandals on the swings.
even though i was just a kid,
i dug a deep pit,
filled it with dreams and heavy feelings,
and hid eternity under my eyelids.

-the new york in me

you're the angel falling from the sky,
with just my voice
to wipe away your smile and
replace it with an all-consuming desire.

i kiss your mouth and
the devil comes out.
i make your eyes roll and
you can't stand that i destroy your control.

but you taste freedom in me.
you come alive, and
that angel who fell from perfection
is the closest to it he'll ever be.

-feelin' love

one look,
heavier than your bass beats, and
you're flying high.
that had you dreaming for a while.

if that wasn't enough,
i whispered something to you,
"i like your music.
it has that evergreen style."

it must've been a spell
because after that,
we fell into obsession hell.
desire crept in and
lit our minds on fire.

tell me about your heart.
tell me about your soul.
what do you love about alaska?
i need to know.
why'd you quit your band?
if you ever see the northern lights,
will you think of me?

i saw you so clearly,
and you tried to forget me.
but always remember,
we saw in each other
the same eternal hunger.

-i know you

i can't get enough of your face.
don't mind me for staring.
i just want to trace my fingers
along your jaw.
who made those eyes and lips?
they're a fucking genius.
you move closer,
bring that face to mine and
i nearly lose my mind.
don't you dare come at me
with those dangerous lips.
you'll destroy me
with your kiss.
i can't remember who i am.
are you real?
what have you done?
it's too much.
your touch...
on my...

-oh my

your gravity pulls at my waters,
but if you are not that lost traveler,
full of passion and virtue,
true and deep,
this is forbidden blue.

so close to you,
i cannot rest.
the movement in me
becomes the tide,
building, spilling.
it's black glass in motion,
dark and cutting.

are you afraid to swim
in unknown depths or
do you have triton's heart?
can you command the
vast and untamed?
then venture into the starlit mystery.
i'll wash over you with savage rhythm,
then wrap you in my silky sheets.

-the ocean at midnight

you treat me like a gift,
something precious and
utterly unique.
you labor in the yard,
build a house, and
put back what falls apart.
don't you mind
my witch's heart?
don't you see
my shadow,
deep and dark?
don't you know
i'm a rose of thorns,
damning and sharp?
all of this you see,
but still,
you plant blackberries
just for me.

-unconditional love

-thank you for reading this collection.

I hope these poems have resonated with you, inviting you to explore the intricate dance between shadow and light. To my loyal readers, your unwavering support means the world to me. And for those new to my work, welcome. I hope you find depth and inspiration within these pages.

For the latest updates and to stay connected, visit my website at www.mercedesparadiso.com.

Your feedback truly matters– if you're willing, an online review would be a cherished gift.

Thank you for joining me on this journey.

MERCEDES PARADISO is an author and award-winning poet with an attorney background. As the author of the poetry collections *Ravens and Romantics* and *Thunder and Daisy*, as well as the novel *Estella and the Dream Traveler*, Mercedes crafts narratives that intricately explore the dynamic interplay of shadow and light. Her work is marked by a lyrical exploration of magic, introspection, and the complexities of the human experience. Living in the San Francisco Bay Area with her family, she continues to invite readers into enchanting, thought-provoking worlds.

-a note about the author